Prayers For My King

Prayer Devotional for Husbands

Prophetess Yokanda Burke

Foreword by Archbishop J. Antoine Miner, Sr.

DEDICATION

This book is dedicated to my first love-The Father, Son and Holy Spirit. Without your loving kindness, I would have never known I was created uniquely for an earthly King, purposed before the foundations of the earth! I would have never learned what love as God intended looks like, what marriage should be and the powerful impact this dynamic creates.

To my earthly King, I pray that God's favor goes beyond your comprehension. That you will live, walk and breathe boldly in the prosperity you are created to reign in. That your heart will always beat proudly and loudly for God: to always love God more than me or anything else. That you will embrace your identity in Christ while surrendering to the Holy Spirit. That you will walk confidently and bravely in your priestly position. That I can help you maintain and sustain the roar of the Lion that resounds in you. That you will always remember that no matter where time takes you, I will always be there as I always have been-praying, warring, supporting, and building you up to be effective for our destined purpose. I love you to life-we shall live to live again my King! In Jesus name, amen!

TABLE OF CONTENTS

<u>FOREWORD</u>

Prophetess Yokanda Burke seems to have captured the very essence of God's divine intention for the Family, the Queen, and her King. Unfortunately, we dwell in an era where the sanctity of marriage is challenged on every side, the divine nature of the "man" seems to be nonexistent, and the roles of the family seem to be rapidly changing. If ever there was a time that this book of divine instruction was needed, that time is now!

This devotional reminds me of the game of chess. I'm often blessed by the concept behind the pieces on the board, more so that of the Queen. Oftentimes when counseling couples, single and those married, I often use the analogy of the Queen on the chessboard. I do this because many women are under the impression that it is only the man's responsibility to cover them. They fail to realize that it is also their responsibility to cover him.

The Queen is the most powerful piece on the board. She is not the most powerful piece because of her radiant beauty. She is not the most powerful piece because she is the smartest. The Queen is the most powerful piece on the board simply because of her KINGDOM responsibility. The Queen's responsibility on the chessboard is to protect her King. She is tasked with the enormous responsibility of ensuring the safety of her King, which intern ensures victory for their KINGDOM.

As a Queen, you have been given the task and mandate to, if necessary, lay down her life for her King. As a Queen on the chessboard, you have more flexibility than your King in your movements of prayer. By your very nature you are a Prayer Warrior, a Strategic Warrior, and a Skilled Warrior.

HER KING TRUSTS HER!

The Bible says in Proverbs 31:11 (MSG), "Her husband trust in her without reserve, and never has reason to regret it".

In Proverbs 31:11, her husband trusts her because she gives him no reason not to. He is confident in her ability to cover him. Because she is a Prayer Warrior, he trusts her source and foundation. He knows that his best interest is in her heart and in her prayers. Her prayers are never for his demise, but rather they are always for his success. She understands that the success of the KING is the success of their KINGDOM!

I encourage every woman to thoroughly read these writings. Do not read them for the sake of reading. Submit to and apply them to your life and your heart. Prayer is the key ingredient to a happy and successful marriage. As a Queen, you are charged with the great task of protecting your King and doing so in prayer.

No matter what the disagreement is naturally, be sure to always deal with it spiritually. As my mother would often say, "TAKING EVERYTHING TO GOD IN PRAYER!!!

Archbishop J Antoine Miner, Sr.

INTRODUCTION

Since the beginning of time, man has been perceived as the head, the forerunners of the world just as God intended. However, after the fall of Adam & Eve, we as a people have forgotten the purpose of our positions, the statutes of our Creator and the meaning of how to live in the Kingdom of God.

The Redemption of Jesus Christ extends far greater than we think or have been taught. Distorted truths brewed by Satan and subtly tainting God's Kingdom has perverted even the simplest instructions of our Father. As Christians, we have allowed our ignorance to produce consequences that we feel we deserve. That as far from the truth as the east is from the west! The Blood of Jesus was shed to restore, revive and restructure all that was misplaced, misaligned and misconceived.

The institution of marriage is the epitome of God's heart. In His Holy Word, we see the importance of it because it's reiterated numerous times. The most profound example I have found is in Ephesians 5:25 (NLT) where it states "for husbands, this means love your wives, just as Christ loved the church. He gave up his life for her."

What greater love is there than this? There's a two-fold blessing here… First, God expresses the core of His heart when he states His love, respect and honor for us even unto death. Secondly, He unselfishly commands us to live likewise! Husbands and wives are commanded to live, love, respect and honor each other just as Christ demonstrated toward us.

I love how God is so clear in explaining His desires to us. In Mark 10:9 (NIV), God indicated: "Therefore what God has joined together, let no one separate." This says to me that covenant is very sacred to Him. If he ordained it, he will stop at nothing to make sure it stays together. No additional persons or things are needed to walk out the covenant God has orchestrated. When we add what wasn't ordained, perversion and distractions are formed. This leads to sin and demonstrating rebellion by turning from His will (as Adam did) and fulfilling our will (self-rule, self-preservation, pride, etc.).

Genesis 2:24 clearly instructs man to leave his parents and stick to his wife like white on rice (I'm paraphrasing). This not only means physically; it also means emotionally, spiritually and mentally. Let me insert a disclosure if I may. I do not wish to offend anyone or seem as though I have the rights of a professional marriage counselor. The contents of this book are solely based on the inspiration of the Holy Spirit and the observations He has shown me through the lives of others. I'm not married yet, but that's because I chose to want what God wants for me and not "do it" for the sake of doing it. I learn by observation and experience alike. I am crazy enough to believe God will direct my husband directly to me when we are both prepared and freed from anything that will hinder our covenant. I'm wise enough to know that growth and maturity are key factors to a strong foundation. I'm not late, I'm well-seasoned (marinated if you will) as a feast fit only for a King! I'm an acquired taste and am perfectly fine with this.

If we look at the church, you don't need statistics to tell you that the divorce and suicide rates are just as high, if not higher than those of the world! Why is this if God created marriage to be a blessing? I have a one word to sum up the entire dilemma-REBELLION! We think God is taking too long, your flesh tells you this is it, you settle because of impatience, you want what you want and expect God to honor it-I could go on and on. The Word of God is not hard to comprehend or live by, it's just that our first nature (sin) keeps getting in the way because we refuse to confront, conquer and control it! I must shout right here and say thank you Father for delivering me from this death trap!

The Bible is littered with instructions on how to follow God's will- are you willing to obey? People love to quote Proverbs 3:5-6 but have no desire of making it a lifestyle. How can God bless our marriage, family, business, government and nations if we won't trust God and His plan for our lives and continue to forget that He's not limited in His Word, actions, promises or power! I had to learn that if God really needed my help, then I could have been on the Cross instead of Jesus. After I accepted Jesus as Lord, that bound me in covenant forever for Him to move in, through and around me as He desires and my opinion is no longer valid!

We must get to the place where we desire God's will and heart more than anything (yes even more than our mates). When we lift God high where he belongs, He'll draw all things associated with our lives to Him. His love will change and compel everyone and everything to flow as He desired the Kingdom to look like in the earth.

Marriage is more than beautiful weddings, kids, building homes and businesses and going to church every week. It's about fulfilling the assignments God has designed for you as a couple. It's about praying and seeking God for everything. it's about demonstrating God's love first in your home then outward to every area of your life. It's about being interdependent with God, your spouse and nothing more. Marriage is bigger than the two of you. Every Christian has assignments and lives attached to us that we are mandated to complete before we leave this earth.

Through your marriage and the activities God has for you to complete, Glory to our King will be manifested!

Wives, we are truly a gift from God to men but I must break your heart and tell you it goes beyond good looks, intimacy and child bearing! Men are called to lead (head). They can't lead if their support system (the spine) is misaligned and paralyzed. As a human birth into sin, we all have issues that stem from a root cause. When we become Christians, the symptoms may seem to have stopped or be hidden, but that's only because the nerve hasn't been awaken again until triggered (maybe by you). Don't think it strange when you see your husband tries to change but can't seem to overcome or you know he loves you but you still feel a gap there. The root causes of these behaviors, issues and distorted truths must be uprooted and burned away by God's Holy Fire!

Please don't try to force the changes, God sees, knows and has a plan! As a wife, we are to be his support system: partner, intercessor, motivator, cheerleader and friend. If they can't come to us as wives naked and unashamed, then we haven't experienced God's love and in turn can't provide it for him until then. God's love is without end-all of the dirt we have done secretly and openly and yet He still loves us the same! We will fall short of God's glory again because His Word tells us.

NEVERTHELESS, we must extend this same grace to our spouses. They may not be Men of Valor yet, BUT THEY WILL! They may not be Men of Integrity yet-BUT THEY WILL! They may not operate in full capacity as God has created them yet-BUT THEY WILL!

The prayers, affirmations, and applications in this book are only training wheels to teach you how to pray for, love and support your Man of God. Married? Not married yet? Engaged? Divorced? Widowed? This book is for everyone. God created that special one for us and though we went through many trial errors, His Word will perform all that He set it out to do concerning us. I pray this book will not only help the man in your life but that you will also allow God to prepare and position you to receive His love in unity!

Peace & Blessings!

<u>PRIDE</u>

Pride (prayhd) n.

noun

1. a high or inordinate opinion of one's own dignity, importance, merit, or superiority, whether as cherished in the mind or as displayed in bearing, conduct, etc.
2. the state or feeling of being proud.
3. something that causes a person or persons to be proud
4. Idioms: pride and joy, someone or something cherished, valued, or enjoyed above all others

As Christians, there are two different types of pride- good & bad. The bible tells us we should be proud of our accomplishments we have worked for (Eccl. 13:22). It's perfectly fine to feel a sense of satisfaction when your child goes to college, you get married, buy a house, etc. This type of proud must be demonstrated in humility. Everything a Christian does and has is ONLY because of God's grace, love, mercy and power. When we keep this at the forefront of our minds as we celebrate our accomplishments, this pleases God. John Flavel said it best "They that know God will be humble; they that know themselves cannot be proud".

True Believers are not exempt however from falling prey to "bad" pride just as the world. Pride in my opinion, is one of the greatest sin controlled by the Spirit Leviathan (also known as the sea serpent).

Prayers against Pride

- **Fault finding**
- **Harsh Spirit**
- **Self-preservation (Superficiality)**
- **Defensiveness (Victim Mentality)**
- **Presumption Before God (self-rule)**
- **Desperate for Attention**
- **Neglecting Others**

PRAYER FOR FAULT FINDING

"It is foolish to belittle one's neighbor; a sensible person keeps quiet. A gossip goes around telling secrets, but those who are trustworthy can keep a confidence." (Prov. 11:12-13 NLT)

Lord I come before you today asking you to cover the man of God you've created me for. Lord I ask that you forgive me and lead me to repentance so that my prayers will not be hindered when I come boldly with these petitions on behalf of my spouse. Father, I come seeking the uprooting of Pride. Today, I ask that you uproot, dismantle and burn away every evidence of fault finding my husband may be bound by. Remove the distorted truths he may have that will cause him to see your beautiful world and creation in negative light. Destroy the lies that lead him to believe that he is not good enough or appreciated enough by myself and others. Pulverize the concepts and behaviors that cause him to spew out words of hurt, pain and destruction towards me and others. I command every word curse that has is or will attempt to take root whether it was done to, by or against him to die by God's Holy Fire now in the name of Jesus.

Holy Spirit, do whatever you must to turn his heart to flesh and embrace the depth of your love towards him. Holy Spirit, minister God's love to my husband naturally and spiritually and make it impossible for him to not accept it. Burn away every residue and evidence of old mindsets, feelings and pain that caused my husband to act in this manner. Show him your thoughts, plans and intents for him Father. When others look upon him Father, let them only see you and not his faults or past. Bridle his tongue so that it will be in alignment with your heart and spirit that rules in him. Remove the frustration of searching for his identity and give him clear revelation along with the burning desire to do your will and your will only!

As he boldly accepts the purpose you have for him, let him readily release his plans and remain rooted in his loyalty and love for you. Fix his eyes like a flint Father and captivate him so intensely in your love that he can only see people, places and things as you see them. Teach him Holy Spirit, how to be a man of integrity always. Teach him how to easily accept and correct his faults. Teach him how to forgive others of their faults towards him and others. Teach him how to love as you love not as the world portrays it. Lord, when we look at each other, let us only see a reflection of you and the enormous overflow of your love. Lord as you move in my love, move simultaneously in me. In Jesus name, Amen.

PRAYER FOR HARSH SPIRIT

"People with understanding control their anger; a hot temper shows great foolishness." (Prov. 14:29 NLT)

Thank you, Father for creating my King and I to live, worship and demonstrate your glory in the earth. Forgive us Father of every ill act, word or thought we may have used that caused displeasure to you. Teach us Holy Spirit how to embrace and operate in your love towards each other and in turn demonstrate this to everyone we encounter.

Your Word in Ephesians 4:2 tells us the importance and the instructions for clear communications. Teach us Holy Spirit how to communicate with each other in gentleness and humility. Teach us how to be patient with one another and give us the endurance we need as we grow and mature in every area of our lives. Cause your love to be the glue that keeps us in sync and magnetize us closer to you. When my husband looks into my soul, let Him only see you resting peacefully in the finished product of my purpose. When I look into my Beloved's soul, let me only see you resting in power, dominion and love in the finished product of his purpose. When our children see us, let them only see you resting peacefully in the fruit of your spirit saturated in your love.

Give us the ability to soothe and keep away all the hurt, pain and ugliness the world has or tries to place on us. Use us God to be an example in society to demonstrate what marital relationship looks like from you. We love you Father and submit our lives as a unit to you forever. In Jesus name, amen.

PRAYER FOR SELF-PRESERVATION

Then Jesus said to his disciples, "Whoever wants to be my disciple must deny themselves and take up their cross and follow me. For whoever wants to save their life will lose it, but whoever loses their life for me will find it." Matt. 16:24-25(NIV)

Father, help my husband to repent another root of pride: self-preservation. Your Word clearly states that we must release everything concerning us into your hands so that we may have everlasting life. Father, help him to no longer worry or fear the pains and struggles that accompany our journeys, but rather embrace them as Christ did. Help him to realize that for us to reign in Christ we must suffer as He did. Holy Spirit, assure him that no matter how painful it may be, You are here to soothe, heal and deliver us out of it all-we only need to ask and believe. Help him to embrace his weaknesses and know that in them he is strong because of you. Give him the confidence to denounce pleasing man and even himself to make himself look as something great and perfect in their eyes. Teach him to hold his head up and understand that you and I love him even in his transforming stages. Remove the guards he has erected to prevent past failures, hurts and issues from reemerging and fill him with the assurance that the past will not be repeated as you remove the root and residue of it all. Let him freely venture into the deep again and embrace the love, success and newness that You produce in his obedience to letting go of the old.

Transform his mind and never again let him feel alone, helpless and unprotected. Show me how to assist him in this new perspective of Your love, hope and future for us. We love You and believe these things so done, in Jesus name, AMEN!

DEFENSIVENESS (VICTIM MENTALITY)

Dear friends, never take revenge. Leave that to the righteous anger of God. For the Scriptures say, "I will take revenge; I will pay them back," says the LORD. Rom. 12:19 (NLT)

Father, help my beloved to see and know You as his Vindicator! Remove the stony surface from his heart stemming from past traumas and issues then replace it with Your heart of flesh. Fill him with Your love until He sees out of Your eyes, will and desire. Fill him with Your love until him demonstrating it becomes more important than the air he breathes! Fill him with Your love until there is no question of whose acceptance or opinion matters-ONLY YOURS!

Fill him with Your love until he never again walks, talks or acts in fear, worry, doubt or self-defense again! Uproot anything that may cause him to be defensive in any capacity in the name of Jesus. Seal all portals that would cause the Defensive Stronghold to try and reenter any area of our lives, bloodlines and life's contents in the name of Jesus. Holy Spirit, teach him how to operate in Your discernment-slow to speak, slow to listen, and slow to anger. Compel him to possess the right attitude, response and execution through your wisdom, revelation and knowledge.

Lord, teach me how to accept the vulnerability he shares with me and to love him through it all. Show me how to assist, nurture and love him consistently, intentionally and constantly as he strives to be the Man, Priest and Purpose You've ordained before the foundations of the earth. Thank you, Father for being our protection in every area of our lives, in Jesus name, Amen!!!

PRESUMPTION BEFORE GOD (SELF-RULE)

"That is why the mind that focuses on human nature is hostile toward God. It refuses to submit to the authority of God's Law because it is powerless to do so. Rom. 8:7 (ISV)

Spirit of the Living God, I come before you on behalf of my Beloved once again. I ask that you have a supernatural encounter with him so powerful that the Stronghold of Self-Rule must crumble and blow away in Your mighty wind, never to return in Jesus name!

Renew His mind so that it replicates the mind of Christ. Attract him to obeying Your Word that tells us Your ways and thoughts are higher than ours. Let this truth compel him to always seek and obey You always in every detail of his life. I renounce rebellion in every form from the contents of our lives and serve eviction indefinitely starting now, in the name of Jesus!

Bind my husband to Your Spirit, Truth and Purpose only. Let every idea, connotation and action be aligned with Your Spirit only. Set his eyes like a flint, his soul in submission and his spirit in compliance to You always. Demonstrate this transformation in our marriage, home, ministries, relationships and businesses or jobs. Fill us with the humility and peace of God so that we will never again sin against you by allowing ourselves or anything else to attempt on thinking higher than you. Let thy will be done in earth as it is in Heaven concerning our lives. In Jesus name, AMEN!

DESPERATE FOR ATTENTION

"Beware of practicing your righteousness before other people to be seen by them, for then you will have no reward from your Father who is in heaven." Matt. 6:1 (ESV)

Heavenly Father, I come before you seeking your guidance, love, wisdom and knowledge to fortify my unity and covenant with my husband. Thank you, Father for joining us together. Thank you for promising to keep us together as we stay on the path of righteousness. Change my heart to become more pure, understanding and strategic in loving my husband. Teach us oh God, how to open the lines of communication so that we can help each other in filling the needs and assignments as you intend towards each other. I command the yoke of bondage to be broken and smashed to dust off his neck in the name of Jesus.

Make him more sensitive to your will, way and desire so that he will lead us as a unit on the path of righteousness. Dismantle every distorted truth that may cause him to act out in seeking attention from man and unrealistic avenues. Please remove the people from our lives that don't represent your intent of marriage. Surround us with anointed covenant marriages that represent your Kingdom and shine your light into this dark world.

Help us to follow suit with your blueprint for marriage. Show us what we need to keep our marriage burning hot and bright while glorifying you. Show us how to lead our marriage in excellence so that we in turn can teach others.

Help us to be protective, supportive and accountable to one another with our vulnerabilities, weaknesses and struggles. As a united front always, we know that we shall overcome every obstacle that will come. We love you and believe these things so done, in Jesus name, AMEN!!!

NEGLECTING OTHERS

"Therefore, anyone who knows what is right but fails to do it is guilty of sin." (James 4:17 ISV)

Heavenly Father, I come before your throne on behalf of myself and my husband. I ask that you forgive us of every sin we've committed against you. Lead us to repentance and redemption. Holy Spirit, show us how to correct every form of neglect we have displayed inappropriately. Show us how to honor and embrace integrity, loyalty and consistency in the people, places and things of our lives. Show us how to conquer neglect with each other. Give us the heart and compassion to remain open to one another, seek you in all things and move in excellence and accountability.

Remove the weeds that would cause us to be offensive, defensive and ignorant when you illuminate the areas of our lives that has been and are neglected. Fill us with your love so that we can demonstrate compassion. Renew our minds so that it's as the mind of Christ, able to obey and execute every strategy as you want. Sync our hearts deeper in your heart so that we can fulfill your desires and will only. Succumb us in selflessness, humility, empathy and kindness.

Show me how to work with my husband to conquer this enemy tactic. I ask that you seal and guard our gateways with your Holy Fire so that we will be able to stand, divide and conquer whatever tries to bound, apprehend, distract or separate your plan for our lives as a unit in every area of our lives. In Jesus name, Amen!!!

TIPS TO COMBAT PRIDE

♥ Pray for God to give you the right attitude, response and execution (A.R.E.). It doesn't matter how many times a day or which circumstance you do this in-just do it until it becomes a habit and your nature is transformed to God's characteristics

♥ Ask God to show you the root cause of this problem and how to combat it strategically. We as women can tend to be too overbearing, which only adds fuel to the fire.

♥ In all instances, remain calm, talk in gentleness and loving tones and pray for A.R.E. over both of you.

♥ Speak life. Speak it openly over your husband, home, finances, family, etc. A man needs to know that he is useful (so many have believed otherwise for many reasons). As his wife, you should be his biggest cheerleader even if he isn't there yet-the point is if God seen his beginning and is standing at his end in love, then why shouldn't you do the same. It's already signed, sealed and delivered-you're there to motivate and compel him to stand and finish strong.

♥ Show appreciation publicly and privately. Women tend to like more attention than men-but that's not to say that men wouldn't like to feel this too! He needs to know without doubt that you are in this together and selflessly walking in love.

   ○ Publicly: get out of your comfort zone and do something he loves or has on a bucket list (skydiving, sports games, etc.) even if you don't like it (I don't care for football but I would be

at every game if my husband happens to be a die-hard fan)

○ **Privately: write notes and stick it in his pocket or wallet; surprise him with a picnic lunch at work; take him to a spa (or do it yourself) and allow him to unwind a little. These things may seem small but the small things are usually what matter the most.**

♥ Speak positive affirmations to him (even in his sleep). Let him know who God says he is. Let him also hear what you see him as-let him always be reminded of why he fell in love with you. Remember, kind words tend to melt away the intents of anger and pain.

PRAYER FOR PRIDE

"Pride leads to disgrace, but with humility comes wisdom." (Prov. 11:2 NLT)

Hallelujah to the King of Kings and the Lord of Lords! Thank you for the BATTLE that You have victoriously won through the shed Blood of Jesus Christ. Thank you, Father for sharing your victory with all who believe on the name of the Lord and are freed through repentance. Holy Spirit, raise up and fortify Your STANDARD within us. I boldly stand in the POWER and AUTHORITY you have graciously embedded in me.

Today, I stand and declare that the root of PRIDE is demolished forever from myself, husband, marriage, family and assignments! Every component of PRIDE, die by God's Holy Fire now in the name of Jesus!

> ➤ I sever the root hairs of "FAULT FINDING" reciprocated and projected onto my husband in Jesus name.
> ➤ Every stench and existence of a "HARSH SPIRIT" in, on or around my husband be gone with the wind in Jesus name.
> ➤ Every temptation of "SUPERFICIALITY" demonstrated towards or within my husband, I cancel null and void in Jesus name.
> ➤ "DEFENSIVENESS", I evict you indefinitely by the power of the Holy Spirit from my husband in the name of Jesus!

> ➢ God's will be the center of my husband's portion; all distorted truths that has, is or will attempt to make him "PRESUMPTIOUS BEFORE GOD"- die now by Holy Fire!
> ➢ Every void in my husband shall be filled with the things of God; "ATTENTION SEEKING" from people, places and things I revoke your access in Jesus name.
> ➢ I sever and pulverize the "ORPHAN and ABANDONMENT" spirit (attention seeking) that leeches in any way to my husband's life in Jesus name.

I pierce the scales of Leviathan, the leader of Pride and command you to go in the name of Jesus. I seal our lives and this prayer in the Blood of Jesus, Conviction of the Cross and God's Holy Fire in Jesus name, Amen!

INSECURITIES

Insecurities (insəˈkyoŏrədē) n.
noun

1. uncertainty or anxiety about oneself; lack of confidence
2. the state of being open to danger or threat; lack of protection.

Society has made sure no one has been untouched by this dreadful interruption. Words spoken (consciously and unconsciously) by others, ridiculous medical guidelines, preposterous idealisms of the entertainment industry- all seeds of insecurities. We train ourselves to speak loudly over the dreams, words and whispers of the enemy words of confidence, positivity and hope.

However, when we stand vulnerable before God and the mirror, do we really believe the numerous affirmations we attempt to convince ourselves with? Though we all carry them (some more than others), it is displayed differently in men. Men are quieter about expressing (or acknowledging) their insecurities. This is due to false realities displayed in the media and defamation of character from all forms of relationships (childhood to adulthood).

It's time to kill this stigma that kills the very nature of our Kings! The lies that made them and us as women believe that if they cry or express their pain, this makes them a weak man. We were built with emotions for a reason-so that we can display the heart of God in Earth as it is in Heaven. We have the power to express and control our emotions. We as women have the innate ability to awaken the life choked by weeds in men through our words, actions and responses of love.

Prayers for Insecurities:

- **Control Freak**
- **Overtly Quiet**
- **People Pleaser**
- **Jealousy**
- **Self- Doubt (Don't like or know how to receive compliments)**

<u>CONTROL FREAK</u>

"A man without self-control is like a city broken into and left without walls". Proverbs 25:28

Heavenly Father, I seek you asking to show my husband how to trust you always. Teach him that you have made him the head but all power belongs to you. Teach him how to self-reflect, resolve and be healed from controlling only what you can control. Demonstrate your love for him through me so that in turn he will embrace you and reflect it to others. Fill me with your compassion, words of affirmation, motivation, encouragement and love as I assist in dismantling this death sentence.

I command the spirits of Jezebel and Ahab to loosen the grips off my husband and die now in the name of Jesus! Father succumb him in the nature of power, authority and ruler as you have designed him. Remove the insecurities that confuses him in how to operate in his true position as a man, Son of God, husband and father. Fill him with your peace, rest and joy so that he will embrace and not rebel against your process no matter how long it takes. Give me your eyes, heart, ears and mind to love him through this transformation just as you do Lord. I love you and believe these things so done, in Jesus name, Amen.

<u>OVERLY QUIET</u>

"And the Lord said to Paul in the night by a vision, "Do not be afraid any longer, but go on speaking and do not be silent." (Acts 18:9 ESV)

Thank you, Father for not giving us a spirit of fear, but that of love, power and a sound mind. Lord, help my husband to see, express and embrace who he is to you. Cease and desist the noise inside of him that confuses his knowledge of your identity, power and authority you put in him. Show me how to plant seeds of activation that will bring life to your will and choke out the hidden weeds sent to suffocate him.

Fill him with the confidence to stand for what is right unapologetically. Fill his soul with the power to execute what you've hidden in his heart and resound it boldly through his mouth. As his help meet, soul mate, friend and mirror, help me to assist in bringing out your best in him.

Teach me to love him through your eyes, unconditionally. Teach my body language to match your love for him. Allow my words to come from your heart. Use my responses to match your embedded submission to your embedded authority in him. In all things Father, we give you glory, honor and praise. Amen!

PEOPLE PLEASER

"Whatever you do, work at it with all your heart, as working for the Lord, not for human masters, since you know that you will receive an inheritance from the Lord as a reward. It is the Lord Christ you are serving." Colossians 3:23-24 (NIV)

Lord, your Word says that you have fearfully and wonderfully made us in your image. You have fashioned us to be a part of you, no mistakes made. Sin through our experiences and the infiltrations of society has caused us to forget this important detail. It has caused us to question our worth and honestly stand in a stupor when you ask us who told us we were naked?

Father, help my King to realize that the only person that he must please is you. Help him understand that in pleasing you this is the only way he needs to please me. Help me to realize that I please you by always interceding, respecting and submitting to your authority in him for this is what pleases You. Holy Spirit, keep us both connected to your statures so that we can only do, love and hate what You do, love and hate. Help us to never be ashamed to be vulnerable with you and each other, for this is where we find our rest, safety, healing and growth.

Make us resistant to every person or thing that tries to intimidate your authority, credibility and power in us. As we stand vulnerable together before you, demonstrate your transparent love in, through and around us for all the world to see. In Jesus name, Amen!

JEALOUSY

"You desire but do not have, so you kill. You covet but you cannot get what you want, so you quarrel and fight. You do not have because you do not ask God. When you ask, you do not receive, because you ask with wrong motives, that you may spend what you get on your pleasures." (James 4:2-3 NIV)

Father, you tell us in Your Word that no good thing will you withhold from us. You also tell us that You know what we need and your promises to fulfill it are always yes and amen. Expose the roots that would cause my husband to operate in jealousy, strife, envy and greed. We know Father that jealousy never travels alone and the longer it is left unattended, the more toxic it becomes to our lives.

Holy Spirit, seek out every root cause that has or will welcome such evilness. Remove it from our lives and open our eyes so we will know how to defeat it if it shows up again! Help us to embrace Apostle Paul's statement in 1 Corinthians 10:23 that we can do everything, however, everything is not good for us. Father, you know what's best for us, what will help us to thrive and be great for your glory. Show my husband how to combat the many forms of jealousy that rear its ugly head. Show me how to follow behind him sealing every opening, denying access to all manners of evil that follows it. Fill us with the desire to appreciate, respect and love one another wholeheartedly-killing jealousy, envy and pettiness in its tracks!

Strengthen our resilience, endurance and strategies daily so that we can continue to fight and stand string whenever it comes uninvited. We reverence You Oh God. We are glad you are a jealous God that want nothing but good for us. No other God could ever compare or contend against your Sovereignty! Thank you for giving us the strategies, capabilities and Your love to conquer all that rises against this union you have joined together. We love you and believe these things so done, in Jesus name, Amen!

SELF-DOUBT

"For it is God who works in you, both to will and to work for his good pleasure." (Philippians 2:13 ESV)

Thank you, Father for giving me such a Beautiful reflection of you! Though he may not always say or show it, I know my King has doubts of his ability to do certain things he's designed to do. Lord, speak to Your Son and show him that You have giving him supernatural abilities to conquer whatever he must face. Thank you for filling him with unexplainable wisdom, revelation and strategies to excel in all he does.

Lord, I know that in order for him to be the greatness You've designed him to be, I must be the balm and support he needs to help him on this journey. Switch my eyes and heart for yours so I can see beyond what is in the natural and decree the manifestations of your promise into existence. Give me the words, strategies, energy, endurance, wisdom, discernment and love to overcome self-doubt, timidity, coy and disbelief of who you created him to be. Show him a new level of humility- allow him to embrace the praises you place in my heart and mouth for him. In turn Father, let him glorify you more for thinking highly of his worth.

As I build his confidence, show him how to build my confidence and together we will boldly walk in the rulership we are destined to. I trust you in all things. In Jesus name, Amen!

TIPS TO COMBAT INSECURITIES

Thanks to society, we inadvertly build cities within us of insecurities that it becomes prevalent in our behaviors. Again, when you have a firm relationship with Christ, embracing who you are as you are becomes easier. It's not our jobs to perfect our or anyone else's imperfections, it's God's. It's also not fair to judge someone's version of insecurity because you have no clue how hard it is to overcome no matter how simple it may be.

- Learn to love yourself as God loves you. As you embrace this, God's glory will transform you and display your growth to all. As you embrace this, your King will relax more and in turn know that he can trust you to accept him as he is.
- Stop trying to fit a mold you weren't built for. So, what your friends Sue and Jim have relationship goals the world qualifies. Your destiny is just as, if not more, important than theirs! This isn't a competition race, it's a work in Truth until I return race. Only what you do for God will be rewarded. As you help set and execute the plan for your marriage, your husband will agree and the benefits are worth it!
- Accept where you are while working towards your destiny! No one wants the flaws we carry, but complaining and comparing won't change it! Set realistic goals as one and work towards it. If you don't finish at the deadline so what. Stay flexible, keep working and encouraging each other through it.
- Learn from life and own it!!! Don't focus on the mistakes, focus on the lessons that will prevent a repeat of the mistake. Remain teachable and focus on

39

staying open to improvement and new things. Encourage your King to keep pushing and reinforce how proud you are of him.

- Display your love and support for him. No matter how small the achievement and growth, reward him with gifts of encouragement such as love notes, trinkets themed for the moment, special treats (um, I'll leave that to your imagination).

PRAYER FOR INSECURITIES

"Finally, be strong in the Lord and in his mighty power. Put on the full armor of God, so that you can take your stand against the devil's schemes. For our struggle is not against flesh and blood, but against rulers, against the authorities, against the powers of this dark world and against the spiritual forces of evil in the heavenly realms. Therefore, put on the full armor of God, so that when the day of evil comes, you may be able to stand your ground, and after you have done everything, to stand..." (Ephesians 6:10-13 NIV)

Thank you, Father for your everlasting and merciful love you continue to show us every day. We are determined to pursue after you hard as one, but we can't do it on our own abilities. Holy Spirit, we give you all rights and access to govern our lives as you desire. Breathe a fresh wind into us oh God. Push out every toxicity that will try to make insecurities govern over us. Whatever the head says the body will follow.

So, Father, I ask that you anoint, protect and renew my King's mind continuously to align with Your desires. Fill me with compliancy and submission to follow his lead as he follows you. We know that all things work for our good because we are love you and called according to your purpose.

> ➤ I decree that when my King speaks, the authoritative roar of the Lion of Judah will be heard, received and respected by all who hear.

41

- I decree that my King walks boldly in his position with his head held high.
- I decree that my King will see me as his Queen and treat me as such always.
- I decree that I will respect, acknowledge and be helpful (not a nag) to my King.
- I decree that my King and I will remain teachable and humble as we are led to push one another into greatness.
- I decree that my King and I are anointed, favored, position and prospered to receive and distribute unlimited wealth in our hands.
- I decree that the strong battling angels will always be on guard fighting every form of insecurity from entering in our divine union, ministry and purpose.

No matter if it doesn't look, feel or taste good, help us to stand fast and focused so that we will one day see the good of your works manifested in us. As you use us to push one another into our destined place, let us remain in love and see it as growth pains and not intentional hurts as our past tries to remind us. Holy Spirit, we believe that you are washing us in the confidence, boldness and tenacity of Christ through his Holy Blood. We love you and thank you for our deliverance, in Jesus name, Amen!

ABANDONMENT

Abandonment /əˈbandənmənt/ n. (noun)

"the action or fact of abandoning or being abandoned."

We were born with the innate ability to create (art, have children, survive), however, nurturing and managing what we create is a learned process. This learned process varies depending on your personal life experiences, traumas and fears (creating distorted truths). The result of this produces abandonment of some sort and many other dysfunctional behaviors.

Men experience abandonment from their mothers and women experience rejection from their fathers (each gender experience both issues, yet at a more heightened degree than the other). The "learned process" our parents expressed were a result cycled from past generations and traumas. No one paid attention that this is wrong. No one said I know this is wrong and I can be the one to change it. No one thought it would affect the child because after all, we all have our own paths to make and take... It's a proven fact that we need to be nurtured, loved and feel safe to recreate healthy relationships. Ever wonder why we subject ourselves to things not right for us (knowingly or unknowingly)? Ever wonder why we feel stuck in situations we know are not good for us? Ever wonder why one little instance can erect a barrier because it reminds us of a past hurt, trauma or issue we'd rather leave in the past or thought we were free from?

ABANDONMENT...instead of treating each new relationship or situation based on now, we tend to base it on past experiences. We don't allow ourselves to receive the goodness of it because if I open too much, I'll get hurt again and I can't go through that again… I've learned from experience and observation that men suffer this type of dysfunction more than women.

No man is born to be a whore, prick, selfish or close minded. It's the learned process that makes them this way. Yes, their mothers may be nice, but at some point, in their lives she wasn't there as consistent as she should have been for whatever reason (I'm guilty of this) causing a void to form in him. Yes, his mother may have been cold-hearted in whatever way (for whatever reason) and left him to figure out only what she could impart into him. He goes through life trying to fill this void in many relationships, not knowing it's his mother's attention, affirmation and love he's seeking.

Every failed relationship causes him to place another layer of sealant over the erected brick wall, creating this man with unhealthy behaviors that simply needs his mother's love. If he only forgives and gives it to God, he can be healed and able to love you as God intended… Now do you understand why he can't love you as he desires, trust you as he desperately needs to and stand as the King he's created to be?

Men internalize while we verbalize. It's harder for them to acknowledge, release and move on. It's even harder when we nag them about doing so. Our role is to help him in the healing process not make it worse. God has given us the ability to speak to every dead area within him to awaken the King that is him!

Words of affirmation, understanding where he is and what God plans as the end result, patience in the breaking and molding, constant sincere prayers and acceptance through this process are the elements that allows him to confidently accept his crown and rule on his throne! It's not easy, but it's worth it. Hang in there Queen, connect with a support system that sincerely ungird and support God's vision for your lives & rejoice in your King's coronation!

Prayers for Abandonment

- **Reenacted Trauma**
- **Unworthiness**
- **Overemotional**
- **Distrust**
- **Self-Sabotaging Relationships**

REENACTED TRAUMA

"But whoever listens to me will dwell secure and will be at ease, without dread of disaster" (Proverbs 1:33 ESV)

Father, I come before you on behalf of my King. Lord, help him to understand that he may not receive the answers he needs as to why traumas, hurts and pains have happened to him. Help him to search within, realize that he can only change the outcome by forgiving the accusers, forgiving himself and being okay with never getting a direct answer on this side of the Jordan as to why it all happened in the first place.

As he forgives Father, immediately erase the memories, pains, behaviors, hurts and stigma that left a huge print in his life. Wash him anew in your healing, soothing, balm of Jesus's Blood. Use me to help him heal, move forward and embrace the Man, Priesthood, Kingship and Mantle you have purposed in him.

Give him the boldness, power and tenacity to cast down every instance now & in the future that will try to remind him and undo the healing you have completed. Give him the boldness to stand as an advocate against that which once held him bound and oppressed for others. Give him new eyes, strategies and ideas to combat this detriment that plagues others in this world.

Fill the depths of his soul with a love, smile and joy that only you can replenish. We glorify you now Father for however you choose to perform this amazing miracle. We love you Father and dare to believe these things & more so done in Jesus name, Amen!

UNWORTHINESS

"Since you are precious and honored in my sight and because I love you, I will give people in exchange for you, nations in exchange for your life." (Isaiah 43:4 NIV)

I come before you Lord with a humbled heart seeking your guidance for my King. Help him to see how much you love him. Help him to see that he is worth more to you than any bird or ruby. Help him to see that because you love him, there will be nothing he can ever do to change how you see him or the plans you have in store. Lord, as your representative of love in the Earth, let him see, embrace and accept your love you pour out of me.

Let him no longer see or feel as though he's inadequate, worthless, useless or less than anything you've created him to be. Teach me how to be patient with him as you continue this refining process. Teach him how to breathe, relax and let control go as you complete the process.

As you walk us step by step through your glory, help us to grow stronger in you, closer to each other and more confident in the purpose you have purposed before the foundations of the Earth. We love you and believe these things so done, in Jesus name, Amen!

<u>OVEREMOTIONAL</u>

"Search me, God, and know my heart; test me and know my anxious thoughts." (Psalms 139:23 NIV)

Lord, I thank you that your love us with an everlasting love! Thank you for creating us to be unique individuals with self-controlled emotions. Help us Holy Spirit to remember that we have authority even over ourselves to command it subject to the control of the Holy Spirit. Show us how to work through the emotions and reactions it creates.

Remove the anxiety that riles up his emotions outside of your character in him. Search my King's heart so that he can come forth as gold after you have tried him in the fire. Help me to stay in my position, give him the space he needs, communicate without condemning him and allow him to deal positively with the things that trigger his emotions in a negative way.

Whatever obstacles he faces, help me to do whatever you need me to so that he can break free of any dark force sent to destroy that which you've built. Let us not forget that you are the only one we're allowed to have control over us, not our emotions. On this day, I surrender our lives to you and believe that you will provide the perfect balance; the balance that will glorify you and advance your Kingdom. In Jesus name, Amen!

DISTRUST

"But let him ask in faith, with no doubting, for the one who doubts is like a wave of the sea that is driven and tossed by the wind." (James 1:6 ESV)

Father I thank you for the opportunity to present my petition for my King before you. Your Word said how can two reasons together unless we agree. How can we trust you with all our hearts & be skeptical of the people that you send to display your trust? Father, I ask that you remove whatever root causes prevent my husband from trusting without reserve and be open to your Holy Spirit's discernment. Help him to understand that you will never allow someone to harm us and if something would cause us discomfort you will make certain that it works out for our good.

Remove the scales from his eyes and allow him to see as you see so that he can live in the peace & rest you so freely give us. Remove the residue of everything that will remind him of negativity and cause him to allow the enemy to push him away from that which you called. Use me first Lord to demonstrate your love through submission, trust and loyalty to him. Use others to demonstrate that in all relationships you have attached to him, your love, loyalty, trust and respect is ever present!

Help him to identify and discard those that mean him no good and cherish the ones that do. Most importantly Father, let him understand the depths, width and breadth of your love so that when he says, "Lord I'm yours", it won't be

50

just lip service but heart service as well. I love you and believe these things so done, in Jesus name, Amen!

SELF-SABOTAGING
RELATIONSHIPS

"Those who disregard discipline despise themselves, but the one who heeds correction gains understanding. Wisdom's instruction is to fear the Lord, and humility comes before honor." (Prov. 15:32-33 NIV)

Lord, I come before you in humility, reverence & adoration. I know for a fact that there is no power greater than you. There is no problem too big for you to handle, no devil too strong for you to demolish & no darkness you can't illuminate! By the power of the Holy Spirit, I stand in the authority given unto me and take back the reins of what belongs to me.

I command every spirit under the control of Python, Leviathan, Jezebel, Athaliah and Herodias to come out of my husband and sons in the name of Jesus. Spirit of Sabotage, Destruction, Confusion, Hindrance, Blockage, Dumbness & Ignorance die by Holy Fire NOW in the name of Jesus! No longer will you control his mind or any other part of his being again. I command the angels to go forth and place a protective barrier around him. As they seal the perimeters of his territory, place an invisible dome shield over it so that any backlash, retaliation, or schemes will bounce off and return to sender.

By the power and authority of God, I bind the hands, plans and radars of the enemy to Hell in the name of Jesus. I loose from heaven the fruit of the spirit, heart of God, mind of Christ, his characteristics, attitude, habits and responses to the control of the Holy Spirit. I decree that he shall be awaken and walk in his God-given position as King.

He shall walk upon the heads of serpents and stand boldly against the things not of God. He shall have an open mind, heart and hands to the ways, plans and depths of God. He shall no longer fear the depths of God, the knowing of God nor the purpose of God. He shall be filled with strength, endurance and tenacity to face every assignment, task and obstacle placed before him for his growth and process. I believe these things so done, in Jesus name, Amen!

TIPS TO COMBAT ABANDONMENT

We have all been dropped before in life by people we never thought would do so. It hurt, made us angry and we lied to ourselves saying we would never let anyone in again! Sidebar: If we really stopped lying to ourselves then we would not have endured so much unnecessary sufferings!!! Ok, I'm back. The closer we get to the Father, the more we will realize that no matter who comes or goes in our lives, we are never alone for he is always there with us!

- Seek God for a stronger discernment. Many times, the signs of warning are evident but we're blinded and dumb by illusions tickling our emotions that we can't see or hear. As your King's help-meet and partner, you are to observe, discern and respond (communicate) what the Holy Spirit reveals. Sometimes you may be led to not say anything but intercede so miraculous intervention can take place.
- Pray for past doors of pain, traumas, hurt and distorted truths to be closed and sealed permanently from both of you. This will dismantle any desire and temptation for the spirit of abandonment to slip in.
- Cast down every imagination, thought and response that is contrary to the will of God for your lives. The only way you can know God's will is if you stay in his presence to receive it!
- Ask God to overpower you with his love so that you can display it to each other. The more this happens the closer you will become and the stronger your covenant will withstand the darts of the enemy!

God didn't abandon us after the Garden, Jesus didn't abandon us on the Cross and Holy Spirit hasn't abandoned us in our mess, so don't you dare allow abandonment to win over your marriage, family and life!!! Fight for the rights of your kingdom Queen!

<u>PRAYER FOR ABANDONMENT</u>

"Therefore, confess your sins to each other and pray for each other so that you may be healed. The prayer of a righteous person is powerful and effective." (James 5:6 NIV)

I look to the hills for you oh God. For you are my refuge, deliverer and Savior. Only you can heal us from everything that tried to damage and discredit us. Father, I come seeking your hand today. Demonstrate the power of your cleansing in my King. Remove the stains, torments, behaviors, habits and defeat from the marrow of his being. I have faith that the Blood of Jesus has redeemed, saved and purposed him for greatness!

Fill my King with your spirit of knowing. Knowing that he is loved, freed, redeemed, received and restored by your Word, power and anointing. Father, quicken his soul to know that you have created a safe place in me for him.

Let him know that in his strength he is safe to display his vulnerability, nakedness and weaknesses with me and it not be used against him. Let him know that every time he lies his head on my chest or lap that his secrets are safe, his soul is protected, his purpose and destiny are fortified. Let him know that as his Rib, Mirror, Partner, Queen, Intercessor, Warrior, Heartbeat, Lifeline and Friend is here to walk the extent of our Destiny for your glory!

Show me how to love my King beyond his actions, weaknesses, ignorance, scars and humanity. Let me be a living magnetic example of what you look, feel and think of him. Let your love cover the multiplicity of his sin and kill it

56

in its tracks concerning us, our children and ministry. I love you and believe these things and more so done, in Jesus name, Amen!

REJECTION

"A rejection is nothing more than a necessary step in the pursuit of success" Bo Bennett

Rejection - /rəˈjekSH(ə)n/ noun

- the dismissing or refusing of a proposal, idea, etc.
- the spurning of a person's affections.

Earlier we touched on the effects of abandonment. Although the roots are similar, the behavior is more profound yet often misdiagnosed. Signs of rejection can be as subtle as a person displaying weakness and defeat, hating to be corrected, sense of entitlement or feeling unworthy. Each person and gender responds with this in different ways, depending on the intensity of the rejection and a person's upbringing.

I have endured rejection from a very young age. My parents were divorced when I was around seven years old and before that I don't really remember having the quality time with my dad as my five older siblings did. I remember a deacon from our church coming over bringing me gifts from time to time. My siblings would tell me that he was my dad. I was confused, yet excited to possibly have a dad in my life to share and learn from. He was nice whenever he came over. Most times in church he responded the same, but other times it was as if I was invisible. I remember clearly (no pain anymore when I remember) running up to him after service as I always did happily saying "Hey Daddy"! I would jump up and down hoping he'd lift me up and kiss me as he did the other times. Instead, I was ignored, regarded as invisible literally! He walked past me as if I never said a word. I was baffled in my child mind as to how can he be so loving one day and cold the next. I later found out the answer only to be faced with more rejection...

He was married with a family. I would be considered the bastard child born from fornication and adultery. Up until around the age of fifteen, whenever we'd go back to Savannah to visit my sister, we'd stop by his house to just see him. My so call brothers (his sons) would say that dad wasn't there.

To this day, the truth hasn't been revealed and I have allowed God to heal me, I'm fine if I don't know before I leave the earth. Honestly in my heart I feel as though the father that divorced my mother is my real father. My stepsister and I look just alike. He never said to me that I wasn't his nor did he treat me indifferent, he just wasn't there for me as he was with all the others. I guess you can say I am the definition of the black sheep.

As I went through life, I had to figure out on my own (the hard way) that all my failed relationships were the result of me looking for what I missed in my father. I had a special relationship with God since I was five, but I wasn't always good at hearing him due to my emotions getting involved. The more I allowed myself to get burned by seeking solutions, the more I had the urge to pull deeper into God.

Today, if I was given the option of redoing my life I'd say NO because it is what has led me to find the needs I sought-desiring the depths of God is the only void filler! Now I am no longer timid and silent, I'm bold, naked (vulnerable with a pure heart before God) and unashamed (of my trials, sins and struggles).

It hurts to rehash the situations that rejected you, but if you can push past the hurt it gets better. You will realize that exposing and resolving it brings a sweet balm that heals all wounds! Same rings true for our Kings. It takes time, love, consistency and patience to heal rejection. It may not look as if change is happening but don't give up!

God sees your heart, your King's hurt and the ordained destiny. There will be victory after this! Focus on the small improvements, see him through God's eyes and demonstrate that you are here no matter what. It's all going to work out great!

Prayers for Rejection

- **Cowardice**
- **Lying**
- **Identity Crisis**

<u>COWARDICE</u>

"Don't be afraid of those who want to kill your body; they cannot touch your soul. Fear only God, who can destroy both soul and body in hell." (Matt. 10:28 NLT)

Lord, you are our strength when we are weak. I pray that you will touch the core of my King and create sparks that will never be smothered or stifled again. Awaken my King from his slumber and soothe his throat with your Word. Your Word says that you will write it on our hearts so that we may not forget your steadfast love. Fill his desire to stand tall against injustice without fear.

Change his language so that it matches what you purpose for us. Change his responses so that it aligns with the power and authority you have innated him with. Shift his mind to align with your spirit so he will walk boldly, confidently and humbly as the King, Priest and Father you have ordained him to be. Search his inner parts God and remove the roots of the pain that has crippled his authoritative position. Pulverize it and seal the areas with your Holy Fire-making it off limits for generations to come because of the Blood of Jesus!

Lord, I need your insight on how to position myself so that he can get his roar back; how to respond so that his confidence is strengthened; how to pray and war so that he stands tall in his mantle. Use me as the tool to position your son to his royal state Father. It is so done, in Jesus name, Amen!

<u>LIES</u>

"The LORD detests lying lips, but he delights in those who tell the truth." (Prov. 12:22)

Lord, our desire is to remain pure before you. Forgive us Father for the times we chose lies over truth. Holy Spirit, expose in and around us every distorted truth and combat it with the TRUTH. For you said in your Word that we must worship you in Spirit and in Truth. We must either love you with our whole hearts or choose the enemy-we can't choose both. We never want to hear you say for us to depart from you because we are not your children!

Father, peel back the layers and teach my King and I how to communicate your truth in every area of our lives. Remove our former ways far from us and embed us in your Truth until it becomes first nature. I cancel the plots of the enemy that try to sneak in and cause us to question the trust we have in each other, our marriage and purpose in the name of Jesus! I bind our lives to the control of the Holy Spirit. Only you Father can lead us in the right direction.

Show us how to walk as one in Truth, Love and Forgiveness always. Make us resilient and extend your grace so that whenever we stumble on a pebble, we can quickly bounce back and continue as one. We realize our lives are not our own but it rightfully belongs to you. I trust and believe you will do it for us Father. Amen!

IDENTITY CRISIS

"Show me your ways, LORD, teach me your paths. Guide me in your truth and teach me, for you are God my Savior, and my hope is in you all day long." (Ps. 25:4-5 NIV)

You are our saving grace in a dark world Lord. Forgive us for allowing glow sticks to lead us through the dark when you are the Bright Morning Star that will illuminate our paths. Forgive us for trying to compare ourselves to lightning bugs when you have adorned us in light brighter than the sun.

Forgive us oh God for getting off our throne to crawl on our bellies with the glow worms instead of allowing your angelic beings and Holy Spirit illuminate our entire territories. Holy Spirit, remove the roots that have caused us to operate in illusion and forget who we are.

Remove the cloaking spirits that come to cover your light and fire within us in the name of Jesus. I evict every thought contrary to our God ordained identity by the power of Holy Ghost. Pulverize every distorted truth that brought about our identity crisis in the name of Jesus. Holy Spirit remove the scales from our eyes so we can embrace our nakedness and detest being clothed and cloaked. Engulf us again in your redemptive love so we can embrace ourselves boldly and unashamed with gladness.

When we look in the depths of each other, show us what you see Father and let that be a permanent fixture that

63

keeps our love and covenant ablaze. Show us our identity and never let us forget it again Lord! Use us to help each other see, embrace and respond only to the identity you have given us. It is so done, in Jesus name, Amen!

TIPS TO COMBAT REJECTION

We must tread carefully and strategically when dealing with rejection. If not, we can do more harm and possibly push the soul deeper into despair. I can't stress enough the importance of prayer when a person is battling rejection. Strategy, preparation and execution is EVERYTHING!

- When God shows you the strategy make sure you ask and hear the timing of execution. If it's done off key, it will backfire which leads to more bricks being layered.

- Make sure your posture (heart, soul, mind, spirit & body) is ready to execute the instruction. Be mindful that some strategies may be repetitive and even seem to be noneffective. Nevertheless, do as God says for he has a plan-your obedience is tied to the successful delivery of his plan.

- Remember it ain't (yes, I used incorrect grammar) what it looks like! It may seem to work then for some reason it looks like he's reverting. This is an old trick of the enemy so that you can get off focus. Keep pressing, stay focused and God will get the glory.

- USE YOUR WORDS!!! If we're going to be known for talking all the time, let it be for something good for a change! Affirm your King daily, multiple times in multiple ways. Rejection douses out confidence and assurance so you must be the oil that refills his vessel. Express how much you love him, respect, honor and believe in him. Write a note and stick it in his lunch bag, wallet or leave it on the mirror; text him simple messages; encourage him when he has a project to

65

finish; find unique gifts just to show appreciation; get creative and DO according to what you know he'd appreciate.

You got this girl! Be lead of The Spirit and do according to what you're instructed. We kill rejection at the root in Jesus name!!!

PRAYER FOR REJECTION

"Therefore, there is now no condemnation for those who are in Christ Jesus, because through Christ Jesus the law of the Spirit who gives life has set you free from the law of sin and death." (Rom. 8:1-2 NIV)

Father, I thank you for using me to distribute breaking power that dismantles everything unlike you! I evict and pulverize the root of rejection in our life right now in the name of Jesus! I command the demons and spirits of rejection to die by Holy Fire now in the name of Jesus! I cancel, send static and confusion to the plans, plots, schemes and all its attachments sent by Leviathan, Python and Ahab, Jezebel, Herodias, Athaliah in the name of Jesus!

I bind you to the sender in the name of Jesus! I bind and blind every witch, warlock, soothsayer, medium and psychic sent on assignment against us in the name of Jesus! I plead the Blood of Jesus over our lives and its entirety. I seal every portal in your Holy Fire. I command every door unlike you to be closed and every door ordained by you to be permanently opened.

Every illegal soul tie attached to rejection I renounce it now in the name of Jesus! I loose your love over every dry place in us. I trust you to heal us and embrace the acceptance of you and each other.

Teach us how to accept the safety in you and each other. Shift every dynamic of our lives Father so we in turn can help in the deliverance of others facing rejection. It is so done, in Jesus name, Amen!

ABUSE

verb

/əˈbyo͞oz/

1. use (something) to bad effect or for a bad purpose; misuse.
2. treat (a person or an animal) with cruelty or violence, especially regularly or repeatedly.

noun

/əˈbyo͞os/

1. the improper use of something.
2. cruel and violent treatment of a person or animal.

Unlike the word "pride", there is no good definition of the word "abuse". The media in our current day has a double standard in accepting and rejecting it. It's okay to sing derogatory lyrics defaming women or writing reality show scripts glorifying, oops I meant "justifying" why it's okay for a person to abuse someone else. You're not even safe in virtual reality!

Social media trolls and hackers find ways to defame, bully and scandalize a person and the law has no way to stop it. Abuse is not always visibly recognized either. What about the parents that neglect to engage with their children because their habits are more important? How about the father that beats his family verbally until the kids grow to believe the lies? What about the words of death that circles around you from the bullies in your life?

Yeah, it may have happened a long time ago, only once or as a joke, nevertheless, it's still ABUSE!!! Abuse is as sneaky as the serpent. It creeps in then have you believing that it's the norm, it has expired or since you ran it has no control anymore. LIES WE TELL OURSELVES!!! If it has never been dealt with head on, then it's lying dormant and behaving subtly or boldly with us.

Don't believe me? Remember the last time someone "commanded" you to do something (that wasn't out of order) and you boldly rebelled? Yeah, abuse rose up. How about when the bully from high school reminisced on how they treated you while at the class reunion and you said nothing? Yeah, abuse still has control. One more…When you watch these perverse, degrading reality shows, movies and music and enjoy it…ABUSE IS ONE OF YOUR STRONGHOLDS!!!

This used to be my life and it took me years to finally be bold, embrace who I am and refuse to accept it anymore! Abuse becomes something you just end up doing even though you always said you'd never do it. It laughs in your face and mocks you to the point that your identity is no longer clear. I can say honestly that I see this played out in my family from a child, cried to God about it and still did nothing to change it until now. Why? Because the enemy made me believe that it was nothing I could do.

I'm so grateful that as I desired more of God, he revealed more of himself in me. He told me that I had to be the change so that the others can change. As I continue to walk on His path instead of Stronghold Boulevard, I have the power to demolish that road piece by piece!

Let me be very clear…IT'S NEVER OKAY TO ACCEPT ANY FORM OF ABUSE ESPECIALLY PHYSICAL!!!! Mental and emotional can be reversed once you make up your mind to seek God and obey whatever he says even if it means separating from the toxic relationship. Physical abuse will eventually get worse if not delivered and you can't save your marriage, fulfill your destiny and purpose if either one of you are dead!

I am not encouraging divorce because I'm not authorized as a doctor or counselor to do so. If this is the case I pray God will lead you to the right resources to deliver you both from this evil. I believe the power of God is strong enough to transform and restore what he has ordained, that's why I keep stressing the importance of seeking God for yourself. Pray, follow the strategies, prepare and execute as led by Holy Spirit!

Symptoms of ABUSE

- **Reserved**
- **Emotionless**
- **Clingy**
- **Unrealistic outburst to simple agreements**
- **Doubt (of love and trust in their partner)**

PRAYER FOR ABUSE

"But I tell you, love your enemies and pray for those who persecute you," (Matt. 5:44)

Father, you are the epitome of love! Your Word says that you only desire good and not evil for us. Lord, how can we receive your love if the stains, strains and habits of abuse rule our lives? We choose you on this day Father to reign indicatively in our lives. We serve eviction to the Spirit of Abuse from our lives in the name of Jesus.

Holy Spirit, do a clean sweep and remove the root hairs, memories, stench, residue and habits of abuse from our lives in the name of Jesus. Every place you clean, fill and seal it in the Blood of Jesus. Every place you excavate the poison of abuse, fill it with your love and seal it in your Holy Fire. Change our taste and desire for the former things unlike you and make it repulsive and foreign to us. Give us a supernatural experience of your love so that we can never forget nor want anything less than it.

Father, you know what is needed so guide and send provision for your will to be done in our lives. Make it impossible for us to not accept it either. Remove resistance to your change for us Lord. Let your love seep from our pores and ooze naturally, consistently and continuously in our lives. Use us to demonstrate your love as one in our homes, businesses, ministry and everywhere else. I believe it so done in Jesus name, Amen!

TIPS TO COMBAT ABUSE

Again, I'm not licensed to give advice or medical diagnosis. The power of the Holy Spirit within me urges you to seek him for guidance on the appropriate steps to remove the root of abuse. Search your local directory for anonymous hotlines, professional counselors, your Pastor and shelters if needed.

- You are not to blame for your abuse. Do not take this guilt because no one has the right to violate another person or animal in any way.
- Do not allow the abuse to rule your mind. You are overcome by the Blood of Jesus! He's forgiven you so now you must forgive them and yourself.
- You must come to the acknowledgement that you may never get an apology or explanation as to why you were the victim of abuse and be fine with this decision. Many times, God will allow this to happen because it is not as important as your destiny!!!
- Never stop praying, trusting and pursuing God. The more you do this the easier the healing process is.

May the favor of God saturate you so much that abuse turn into affection, respect and honor from your King in Jesus name, Amen!!!

ANGER

Anger

/ ˈaNGgər/ noun

1. a strong feeling of annoyance, displeasure, or hostility.
2. fill (someone) with anger; provoke anger in.

Personally, I do not think the definition fully explains the toxicity of this word. It reminds me of the epitome of Satan's reaction to being caught then thrown from Heaven to Earth. He wanted to be God so badly that instead of him competing in a good way to prove he is more loving than God and worthy than Jesus, he used his reign to taint, destroy and kill only the things and people of God.

Anger never acts alone of course. Satan and the angels he manipulated are the same way and won't stop until there's nothing left! Greed, envy and jealousy are the ride or die partners that make sure they accomplish their goals.

It starts as a seed subtly planted then festers like a tightly closed jar filled with chemicals and left in the sun for many hours. It eventually is going to bust loose and damage whatever is in its wake! Society has taught us that we are to hold in our frustrations, do as told and show strength at all times. How absurd! If we were meant to be robots, then we wouldn't need emotions or a soul.

The Word tells us numerous times the importance of not indulging I anger for the consequences are detrimental. Yes, anger is one of the emotions God embedded in us, but it never was intended to be used to harm us. Ephesians 4:26-27, states "In your anger do not sin: Do not let the sun go down while you are still angry, and do not give the devil a foothold." God is telling us to communicate this anger in love and settle it before the day is over; if not this gives Satan the invitation to come in and plant weeds that will choke out the Word and grow explosively like the plant from the movie "Little Shop of Horror"!

If your King struggles with anger, pray about it then try to communicate with him so you can agree to a strategy that will dispel it (this goes both ways). The depths of anger are sometimes hard to find. Seeking knowledge and strategy from Holy Spirit will end your scavenger hunt to reclaim your King's victory.

PRAYER FOR ANGER

"Get rid of all bitterness, rage and anger, brawling and slander, along with every form of malice. Be kind and compassionate to one another, forgiving each other, just as in Christ God forgave you." (Eph.4:31-32 NIV)

Father I trust that you have a plan and purpose for us. I trust that you will heal and deliver us from everything that tries to attack our divine covenant. Holy Spirit, I give you full authority to intervene and bring vindication to us! I command the Stronghold of Athaliah and every spirit and demon under her power to die by Holy Fire never to return to our lives in the name of Jesus! I cancel every plan set, thought and here null and void in the name of Jesus!

Holy Spirit, use me to dismantle and siphon the roots, weeds, stench and residue of anger from my King. Fill me with your wisdom, knowledge and discernment to cover, protect and love him through the deliverance. Rapidly demonstrate your manifested power working in, through and around us so that our marriage will glorify you alone! I believe it is so done, in Jesus name, Amen!

TIPS TO COMBAT ANGER

I know y'all might get a little salty with me right now, but one of the best combats would be to just shut up during the height of a situation. If you keep giving tit for tat, nagging, whining and complaining then guess what- you're just as responsible for the wildfire as he is. Learn to humble yourself and take it to God. Not everything requires a battle and not every battle you will be captain over.

- Don't reciprocate what is thrown at you. If he's shouting, don't shout back. Instead respond in love and/or wait until he calms down to have a reasonable conversation about it. Remember anger is triggered by another underlying germ so put on your spiritual eyes and look again. This will help tremendously in the results

- If something simple triggers him-do your best to not do it. Nothing is worth putting a tear in your undefiled bed so learn to be flexible and compliant.

- If you pray for the right attitude, response and execution for the both of you, the dramas will cease and the fellowship will bloom.

- Love stifles anger! Even if he doesn't deserve to be hugged on or kissed now do it anyway. He will begin to realize that you are not the source of his problem and in turn be open to change.

- If anger becomes deadly or hazardous, please seek professional help and remove yourself from the situation. No one's life is worth losing over something that can be resolved eventually.

IRRITABLE MALE SYNDROME (IMS)

"A true relationship is two unperfect people refusing to give up on each other" Unknown

According to a newsletter in Healthline, irritable male syndrome (also called andropause) is the male version of menopause women experience. So, I'm definitely not relieved to hear this really exists but it's true. Symptoms include irritability, lack of concentration and sleep, low sex drive and energy. I believe if you add a nagging wife, this will throw him irritable to agony (poor dude)!

This isn't seen in all men; however, it can explain some of the reasons for the mentioned issues in this book. There are treatments to prevent and assist in easing this syndrome. My favorite one is active deliverance! Queen, you better do what you need to do so that sex drive doesn't turn into depression (of course I mean within the confines of the law set by God).

Seriously, we never know what they battle and the depths of it internally so we must be sensitive to his needs. It can be a scary thing to know that your stability is being shaken and it's out of your control. Be the stability, peace and warmth that he needs to regain control of his throne.

<u>PRAYER FOR IMS</u>

"For I am the LORD your God who takes hold of your right hand and says to you, Do not fear; I will help you." (Isaiah 41:13 NIV)

Thank you, Father, for reaffirming your love and extending your grace to us once again. We know that you hold us in the palm of your hands even when we can't see you. Lord, I ask that you restore balance in us, our home and our lives. I cancel every plan sent to thwart and shake our destiny in the name of Jesus. I place my Kingdom and King in your hands

Father. I trust that you will heal him and restore balance to his being. I command everything in our lives to come into alignment with your will or be far removed from us in Jesus name! The greatest cure is through the power of your Blood Jehovah Rapha! Use me Holy Spirit in his healing process. Show me how to minister, nurture, support and heal my King.

I thank you in advance for restoring your order, purpose and destiny in us again! It is so done, in Jesus name, Amen!

AWAKEN QUEEN, YOUR KING AWAITS!

My beautiful, sexy, unique, favored, strong, graceful, destiny filled sisters- I call you forth to reign as Queen as one with your King!!! Arise, get in position and do the work of a Queen. There are many women in the Bible that weren't Queens, however, the postures they held were regal, powerful and the driving force that awakened her King and intensified his roar! I want to help you bring the best out in your marriage with tips that can ignite and assist in keeping the flame steady. None of these tips are mandatory, meaning find what works for you. Whatever you choose to do, make sure that YOU are comfortable and open enough with yourself to do it and do it proudly.

- Pray without ceasing for your King but also for yourself. Everything won't be about his change alone, it's a joint effort.
- Love him through his process wholeheartedly. Make sure to keep the lines of communication open, listen to what he is saying and respond based on reality not emotions. If you have a strong prayer life, Holy Spirit will teach you how to communicate effectively.
- Be open to new ways of spicing up your relationship. Communicate and agree upon limitations, try them and discuss what works and what doesn't. Remember, you will be together for life and I'm sure you don't want to do the same mundane routines every single day!
- Take more care of your temple. This shows God and your King that you honor and appreciate it. I'm sure

he will love to see variety and the benefits of it. Throw away the granny panties, sweats and bulky loungewear; wear lingerie (or just you); start a new skincare regimen to supple your skin; decide together and buy some new toys to spice up your bedroom ministry (seriously, intimacy with your King is a ministry); take vitamins and supplements; exercise (yoga, walking, cardio, pole dancing, whatever floats your boat).

- **KEEP EVERYONE OUT OF YOUR PERSONAL BUSINESS EXCEPT GOD & YOUR KING!** If God wanted people's opinions guiding your marriage, he wouldn't say that the marriage bed is undefiled-off limits. If outside advice is needed, he will lead you to someone qualified to do so. This also helps the trust and loyalty to remain strong. You also save yourself from unnecessary warfare sent through others intentionally and unintentionally.

-

Lord I ask that you strengthen each Queen to reign as you intended. Teach us how to embrace the beauty, glory, radiance, uniqueness, grace and favor you have filled us with. Show us how to use our tools to build our Kings and Kingdom up, how to exhibit your love on stage and behind closed doors and how to seek your face for everything we need.

Thank you for choosing our Kings and counting us worthy to be bone of his bone and flesh of his flesh. Lord, we can do none of this without you. Lead, guide and nurture us as we walk tall on this challenging road all for your glory. We thank you for teaching us the right way of covenant so that we in turn can teach our peers and children-spreading your Truth like wildfire, shifting the dynamics of the Earth! We love you and believe these things so done, in Jesus name, Amen!

I want to thank you for taking this journey to living in covenant bliss as God intended. Will everyday be gumdrops and rainbows? No, but it will be worth it when you are walking in your destiny and purpose as ONE. As children of God, we are to always demonstrate His will in the Earth. This must first start at the core-our marriage.

When our marriage is aligned, everything else MUST fall in line with the plan of God. Enjoy this process as you both go as one growing, learning more about yourselves and each other and thriving gracefully.

Whether you know it or not, the world is watching you because the glory is on your life. Represent our Father well and you will never regret it!

BOOKS BY PROPHETESS YOKANDA BURKE

Heart of a Worshipper: 45 Day Prayer Devotional

3 CORD STRAND SERIES

Prayers for My King

Prayers for My Queen- coming soon

3 Cord Strand: Not Easily Broken- coming soon

WARFARE SERIES

In Dew Time-coming soon

Beyond The Travail-coming soon

It's Morning Time- coming soon

NOTES

1. **Bible Hub. 2004-2016. 29 June 2017.**
   www.biblehub.com
2. **Google Search Engine is where the following definitions are derived:**
   a. **Pride.** http://www.dictionary.com/browse/pride
   b. **Rejection.**https://www.google.com/search?q=reje
      ction&rlz=1C1CHZL_enUS747US747&oq=reject
      ion&aqs=chrome..69i57j0l5.2227j1j7&sourceid=
      chrome&ie=UTF-8
   c. **Abuse.**https://www.google.com/search?rlz=1C2C
      HZL_enUS747US749&source=hp&ei=bvsOW6e
      OIcvC0wKA-
      q0I&q=abuse&oq=abuse&gs_l=psy-
      ab.3..35i39k1j0j0i20i263k1j0l7.1347.2294.0.2630
      .6.5.0.0.0.0.189.892.0j5.5.0....0...1c.1.64.psy-
      ab..1.5.889.0..0i131k1j0i131i20i264k1j0i67k1j0i2
      0i264k1.0.78gmiILKjVk
3. **Graham, Billy. Answers. Web Article. Dec. 9, 2015.**
   https://billygraham.org/answer/can-pride-be-a-good-
   thing/
4. **Harford, Fabienne. Seven Subtle Symptoms of Pride. Web Article. July 15, 2015.**
   http://www.desiringgod.org/articles/seven-subtle-
   symptoms-of-pride
5. **Smith, Stephen. OpenBible. Feb. 1, 2018.**
   www.openbible.com
6. **Tarrants III, Thomas. Knowing & Doing. Web Article. Winter 2011.**
   http://www.cslewisinstitute.org/Pride_and_Humility_Sin
   glePage
7. **Mark, Licensed Marriage & Family, L. (2017, December 01). Common Abandonment Issues for Men -- A Mother's Impact. Retrieved March 18, 2018, from**

https://seattlechristiancounseling.com/articles/common-abandonment-issues-for-men-a-mothers-impact

8. Rowett, A. (2017, March 31). 7 Most Common Abandonment Issues Symptoms. Retrieved March 18, 2018, from https://seattlechristiancounseling.com/articles/7-most-common-abandonment-issues-symptoms

9. Roland, J. (2016, December 19). Irritable Male Syndrome and Your Relationships (T. J. Legg PhD,CRNP, Ed.). Retrieved May 30, 2018, from https://www.healthline.com/health/mens-health/irritable-male-syndrome#symptoms

10. Villalon, C. (n.d.). Home. Retrieved May 30, 2018, from https://inspiringtips.com/ways-to-overcome-insecurities-in-a-relationship/

11. How to overcome rejection: Correcting a mistaken identity. (n.d.). Retrieved May 29, 2018, from http://www.greatbiblestudy.com/rejection.php

12. Twigg, N. T. (2016, July 19). 15 Rejection Quotes. Retrieved May 29, 2018, from https://www.thedailymind.com/motivation-inspiration/inspiring-rejection-quotes/

13. Love Inspiration Quotes. (n.d.). Retrieved May 30, 2018, from http://shayariabc.com/20165/love-inspiration-quotes/#